BACKLIT

BACKLIT

William Benton

PRESSED WAFER

ISBN 978-1-940396-26-2
First Edition
PRINTED IN THE UNITES STATES OF AMERICA

PRESSED WAFER
375 Parkside Avenue, Brooklyn, NY 11226
www.pressedwafer.com

For Natsuko

Yet they had met,
Friend and dear friend and a planet's encouragement.

—Wallace Stevens

CONTENTS

I.

II.

I.

THE RAIN DRAGON

I'm the one who has imprisoned the rain dragon.

You know the story? About the dark-eyed girl who seduces
the holy man and ends the long drought.

The cage where he keeps the rain dragon is a waterfall.

Your hair is a waterfall and distracts me; I lose all sense
of my avowed purpose – the dragon escapes.

It rains and rains.

DINNER

Candlelight burnishes
her plum sweater.

An odalisque, an ode, a no.
An Eskimo.

Gray eyes partly crossed.
Pregnant.
One tooth wasn't perfect in the front.

Grieg's small coins are thrown

from a bag filled
with yellow leaves.

SCIENCE

For Nat

Arranged in a single
cluster, tiny insects

with coral colored wings
mimic a flower.

We knew this because
they survived.

Two things happened: they lived
and at the same time

revealed the veil
of destiny reversed.

They lived like love,
beyond disaster,

in a form entirely
its own proof. Otherwise

all we'd know of them
is mute absence—

nothing—
another branch.

CAMERA OBSCURA

A tiny catchlight of saliva
shows as she opens her mouth.

In the moment of recognition

details of the glitzy room
slip from focus: she stares

out of the shadow of her hat—
a wide-brimmed, red, feathery affair—

aware of what is rehearsed
in the encounter, undaunted,

prepared for that alone.

THE VISIBLE LEAF

You're still at the lab,
with your hair drawn casually back.

Molecules rehearse
an unceasing continuity

in the visible leaf.

It was fun to see Montreux, the surprise
of palm trees along the promenade, the castle

with its endless visitors. I want you to be
a part of the day's attention,

not an interlude, but complicit

in all the intricate
and hapless details

that are the sum,
the unknowable mosaic, the house

that love builds for itself.

IMPASSE

The yellow pinafore flares
side to side. She doesn't

turn her back. Set against
the blank wall of the block

a switch is made without
sounding to bluer depths.

I can't get the ornament
to dance. Things possess

the immediacy of their
sacrifice. The moment

comes to a halt in midair,
a faint mechanical lie.

THE LAWRENCE SNAKE

Their faces shine,
grins dripping, that

came before me to
drink where I drink.

In the stone trough
the rippled surface

returns to a flat plane.
The water flows clear

at an imperceptible rate. What
makes it a woman

in the first place
purifies both. Sunlight

loosens her hair.
You cannot be

the husband of every
happiness, D.H.

THE TIN ROOM

At dinner she makes
an accomplice. Cackles

and peeks from behind
the bones of her fingers.

Filaments of web
settle weightlessly

into place. The movement
of an arm draws

around her a cape
of smoke. Silent,

divided against ourselves,
we leave the restaurant,

baffled by the infallible
performance

that requires now
with her walking

up the street
our pity.

SALTWATER

The light moves like
nerves on the water

white jittery lines
I can see the shadow of
my head its own

dark confusions.

Palms shift in the wind.
We were all silent,

the children aware,
an incalculable

weight, their arms
thin as flutes.

I'm sorry; I can't stay.

She steps onto
the veranda,

beacon, flower,

outlined against
yellow squares

of lattice-work
and the sea beyond

beyond Bonnard.

AWAY

Bright noon,
the narrow stairs lead

into the water, cool
wavering shallows,

she looks at her feet.
The way back had logic,

a maze of marks
in frozen flight

through the gray trees.
Her hair is a wreath

in a story laid
darkly on the pool.

CONCORDANCE

I. MONSIEUR LOYAL

The tirade is over.
He retains a show of menace,

shifting his weight
from one foot
to the other.

I am demolished, nothing,
insubstantial as air.

My stupidity is left
standing between us
like a small black horse.

2. THE GIRL

Every day a man paces
back and forth on the balcony.

His coat leaves a smear
on the glass doors.

It doesn't matter if the will fails:
automatically you reappear,
first as a shadow on the wall,

then your knees, lightly
touching, followed by the rest,
a young girl, nude,

standing perfectly still,
staring at the closed doors.

3. THE FOOL

Authority, wearing the ringmaster's coat,
touches me on the shoulder.

I turn my gaze toward him like a fool.

The tableau fills in behind me: a girl
watching from the shadows (her white
legs glisten in my mind), and
the anonymous man who enters from

the other side. They share the Mercator's
edge where equals meet. My clothes hang

loosely on me. The calliope cranks up.

4. THE LAMP

A six-pack (that glow), skin,
heavy overturned stones of
anguish, and the glint of loss
on walls of polished obsidian:

this is the lamp, the zig-zag
border of its shade. It shines
at the kitchen table's edge,
illuminating the lines

I write in a notebook
or – like a half-formed face
emerging from the dark –
the specter of impasse.

5. TWO MEN

I couldn't pretend he wasn't there.
It changed everything, the ground
in summer, the high-topped weeds.

His placement in the dusty field
lent an air of parable to the scene.
Small in the distance I ran toward

him, crying, Father, O, my Father.
Actually I doubt if I said a thing.
No one else was in sight. Without

stopping I passed him like a fixed
point in the lines of perspective
that composed my view. I walked

for a long time. After a while
a faint swagger began to enter
my stride, a casual bounce.

6. THE COUNTRY ROAD

Beside a low wall
foliage grows

like waves breaking
into myriad points

of spray. Light lingers
evenly in the sky. What

was the backdrop
of an event is now

the event itself.
I can't see it

except for the absence
that is there.

7. THE BALCONY

I watch for you from up here.
The streetlights blink on

in the Paris dusk. Fears

crowd my consciousness: I know
why you don't come.

That part is always the same.
The revelation, each time,

is that you do.

8. TREE TRUNKS

Standing in a row
at the edge of the river,

those trees are the men.
I'm the water. I mimic the way

they look and what they do
in the sliding wind.

ॐ

I take on the mannerisms, voices,
even the thought processes of others.

I despise my skin and can't escape or fully occupy it.
An empty insufficiency

forces me to act. I pool slowly, all
surface stars and self doubt.

ॐ

The row of trunks

in a single motion

rakes through my life.

II.

THE CLIMB

For Joey

I.

The mass of rocks starts at one end of a wide cove,
white sand turns grassy,
a headland rises up.

It seems easy, the gaps and angles
anticipate our steps. He leads the way.
The curve of beach

slips out of sight. We're on a sparrow ledge
high (suddenly)
above the ocean.

2.

Scale vanishes, replaced
by the distance of fall, the feathery
presence of fear.

Below us a diver snorkels
the craggy shoreline.

In the ungiving
configurations,
the density and indifference
of rock,
fear measures itself
separating into
a loose shape,
half air.

3.

Flat against the rock-face
I inch out over a sheer drop,

a fossil gleams

white with dark rune-like lines.

Keep three
positions and move a hand
or a foot.

I feel for a toehold
and find nothing.

Letting go would for a moment be
that I'd tossed the earth

into the air.

4.

The downward pull is small

tilting out over the empty
dimpled beach.

From here to here
is a life. A bird's shadow

crosses the rock
and disappears into

point-blank blue.

5.

Water reflects
onto the cliff's

surface a skin
of motion

as we descend. We
can't stay there,

its stern example
overarching and

suspended is too
simple. The conflict

rises before our eyes
like a heap of

rocks or skulls.
We step down,

shadows falling
on a flat plane,

the long way back
in front of us.

THE TRAIN

You're like her, the way she stood
beside him on the railroad platform,

steadfast in out-of-date clothes,
not knowing what it meant

to be there, except that it meant
everything. The green is impenetrable

surrounding the station in
the noon sun. Footprints of

tigers and ruby-eyed birds
inhabit the stillness

as they wait for the train
that will leave her there.

THE DRAWING

Her gown descends limply
over slender hips.
She stands

at the exact center
of the page.
You have to be told

it's Ophelia. In
dry-brush, a pale
ash blue.

The woman
who owns the picture speaks
in opposing tropes.

Autumn can't mean autumn.
The backs of her fingers
spread leisurely

upward through the dark
mass of her hair. She doesn't
agree with me

about Vivaldi. Her
hand remains at her shoulder,
like a pet bird.

Has anyone ever been more vertical
than Ophelia—
the mad unloved girl

upright in an emptiness
that swallows her?
I stood looking at

the picture, flat-footed,
unaware almost of
how I got there.

The face of Ophelia
is familiar to me. I
had come to escape it.

STEPS

They spin like nonsense

and come apart. Men talked
to her at an angle,

thin as reflections during the afternoon.

The blistered drums deprive the momentum
of its comic inertia. A door shuts

and disappears; invisible, innocent,
always a wall.

ARRIVAL

Silhouettes and names,

Leduc's line:

sparrows born in Paris.

Easy, sensuous, the light shifts
from one center to another

exempt from the errors of probability

a ball in the air

that falls down as rain.

WINTER NIGHTS

For Sangmi

Too bad the waste
of these winter nights

can't be saved up, placed
inside the folds

of a counterpane—
a half-remembered thing,

kept in the linen closet—
cut perfectly to fit

by the knife of spring.

THE ARTIST'S WIFE-TO-BE

She's fallen asleep
on one of the plush surfaces
inviolate
in the left-on light
like a light
in a tower. Her face
is still flush
from an occasion
her party dress
and crinolines
attest to, her
unremoved shoes.

The dark background
swirls around her, violent
in its purity – a river
of paint flashing
its scales. Paint
is the boundary
she will have to cross
to be a part
of his life.

This is the figure
who awakens
from the sleeping figure
of herself: a girl
in the pale whites
and mauves of a lover.

Placed close to
the viewer, at the edge
of the canvas,
she looks almost royal,
suspended
in the serene indolence
of being his.

SAGAPONACK NOTEBOOK

For Jim and Kay

Leaves in the wind
rehearse alternatives.

Wind in the leaves.

ॐ

The permission seems
innocent of limits, composed
of proportion.

Blond weeds
edge the pond. The same page
every day.

Which is all there is
I decide,

decisions.

ॐ

Saga.

The voices of geese
travel.

ॐ

East is east.
East diseased.
East deceased.

༄

Tassels soft as mops
     the tops of cane

        flare and go out
    in the low sun, which drops
        behind a mansion

           of someone's.

༄

Let me count the waves.

༄

Long

I'm on that
island

I do.

RIDER

Like the thought
that thought him up

a horn rises
from his head

spiral of animal
smell, a hard-on

for the phantom
lady in the garden

whom he reaches
in one bound

the swift foot
cleft as it touches

the flowered
ground.

REVENANT

Young, nondescript,
well she's a little fat,
the lift and fall of thick
uncombed hair hastens
down the stairs to the train.
Above the East River
dull ochre smoke hangs
night-lit. I never go
to Queens. Loss is diffuse,
the abacus of kisses can't
add it up. The impossible
opposite of every moment.
You feel the stars flinch.

THE JITTERBUG ASHES OF LIGHT

Reflections of water
shimmer on the ceiling.

Outside my room, the bay
is calm. Silver and black

alternate in the crinkled
foil of its shine. The hour

of dusk slips like a mask
into place. On the pier

Aunt Sis sits with her legs
dangling down.

An identity signified
by terms of relation

alone. Crepe myrtle
remains in the air. The lights of

beer joints come on
where my mother dances

from star to star.

THE SAILBOAT

The sailboat belonged to a man named Al,
who lived on our street and worked for
the Post Office as a mail carrier. Moored
at anchor, it sat on the bay like a solitary "I."
Al had an affair with Ann, our cousin,
who was tall and good-looking. The boat,
previously unnamed, was christened Ann,
spelled out on the stern in brass letters.
Al, with his barrel chest and gray mustache,
his desiccated wife Bessie, and Ann, were
a story connected to our lives on the bay.
Years later, after we'd grown up and
moved away, with marriages of our own, in
worlds that almost never met, my brother
made a painting from memory of the boat
sitting on the glassy water at sunset, its
mast the black wick of a great flame. It was
an image he kept in his head, one of many
that he counted like gold, over and over.

EPITHALAMIUM

For John and Melissa

The tapestry that
depicts the capture

is a ragged fragment,
half gone. It shows

only the dogs – the gnawing
pack of desires –

and her fingers in
the white curls

of his mane.

꒓

A slow learner
he had to discover

on the run
that the act was pure

and gave him her
and made them one.

꒓

She goes through lime trees
and white hawthorn,

dragonflies pause
in mid-flight. The silver

weave of prerogatives
flickers its knives.

He approaches the clearing,
the sunlit leaves,

the trampled
rise of earth.

MIDNIGHT

You can see the ocean
smeared with shimmer,

palms chatter in the year
I mean the yard. I'm

a little bit nervous
visited by a presence

of cessation, drinking
beer on the screened-in

porch, the wild shore
the one girl all

that self is
and then is not.

III.

SIX POEMS

FROM

MARMALADE

QUELLE SOIE

What silk
that time.

Mirror
Chimera,

your hair
twists,

intends.
Loopholes

along our street
are raised

like flags.
Glories.

Love,
breathe out

in your cry
and in.

L'APRÈS-MIDI D'UN FAUNE

Three carnations
one black and two red ones are arranged
deftly, drowsy vaginas
aroused by the stems of flowers, awaken the nymphs. . .

Le Faune arrives
on the scene. He pauses
in a small meadow
and rubs his eyes. But what happened was
a great commotion was ensuing, and
an animal whiteness mingled
now with something seen for an instant
it fled through the branches.
Le Faune felt
this was awful. For he
thought the girls very beautiful and wanted
to fuck them. But now they
were gone. So, at length, he closed his eyes,
to sleep in the soft grass of the meadow. And
one by one, the beautiful girls
took shape in the dark of his eyes.
For a time
he loved the dream. Yet it caused him
to look again forlornly at the empty meadow.
He had, he knew, but one hope which was to chase
into the forest after the beautiful girls. But
then he wondered, *which forest?* Now,
there were two forests,
and one was real and one was
the other one. Le Faune was so confused
that he didn't go into either of the forests. He went
to a little garden
bordering on the meadow. And there
he sat down and offered
to himself, as a small triumph,
the ideal lack
of roses.

Poor Le Faune set about ordering his thoughts.
He wanted to follow the beautiful girls.
He thought of the two forests, each with silver
and black leaves, surrounding the garden.
Where, where, where was the nature of his hard thoughts.
Where did they go? He scratched his head.
Oh no, cried Le Faune out loud. Not in *there*, he
protested.

But they were.

Well then if that is so pondered Le Faune,
and he forgot
about the two forests, shimmering in the sunlight
assuming wrongly that the journey was to be
unfraught with complexities, and that soon
safe inside his own head he would find only
the beautiful girls. How could
he have known differently? There was no one
to tell Le Faune. But then
he chanced upon a Weeping Spring in the woods.
Actually
it was somewhere in between the real woods and the
other, but when Le Faune came upon it it wept
from blue eyes
which, he realized, were his own,
and he wept too. Sadly
he saw the journey had begun and he was lost.
Oh, well. He would speak to the Weeping
Spring with the twin-pipes
of his flute. He was surprised, hearing
the notes turn into a lovely song, uncomplaining
because here
the music floated on the water
and he had become himself the Wind having traveled
a little bit. Thus encouraged, he went on in his song
about the Water and the Wind and the Trees
saying that those things came to exist because
this was that song
in which they were inspired sort of like it was, which
it said,

regained the sky.

Sitting under the sky, Le Faune saw what had happened.
He was back in the little garden, at the edge of the
meadow.

Capitulating, he mused upon his adventures:
I was pretending to be
the sun, up over the flowering world
a moment ago.
Just then the light
brightened all about him
and he saw that the white flowers, growing
from the earth, had become precious to
the sunlight. It was a quest
not unlike his own, as the sun glanced off
the white bodies Le Faune saw
in the flowers. Sun woke them.
And they fluttered away, like naiads.
That was the *song* he had heard,
when he spoke to the Weeping Spring!

Thus, the journey returned to Le Faune. He felt
the song stalking him
like a traitress, dressed in a raiment
woven of leaves.

From his death,
Le Faune entered again
the glittering woods. All around
him the leaves parted, and there on a small hillock
were the beautiful girls. His mind
played quickly over the two sisters awakened
by the red flowers
and they met, entwined by embraces, as his mind rose
over them and up to the place where, it seemed,
the sun was. The powerful black carnation
of his mind grew like a star
on the sun's face. And Le Faune picked up
the twin-pipes. He wanted only to play a single note
from the intricate design of the song which the sun
knew. It was *la*. And it was the note in which the escape
of the beautiful girls took place
in the song. As he played it, he knew
also that it was the note in which no one could ever
know the secret of how the beautiful girls always had fled.
He played, it was
a long solo, proud of its noise, wrested
from the silvery-black husks of leaves
luminous in the evening sky.

So that is how, in the note, they escape.

From his lips.

HÉRODIADE

A blackbird flies

into the day, extinguishing stars.

༉

It's a crime the sky had to be purple.

NO SPLASHING!

signed,

The Purple Accomplice.

༉

On the wing of a vanity
a bottle of Old Snows effaces the tacky giltwood.

The red window, wide open.

Her ideas
bunch into flowers. Their long stems and regret.

A lone vase. Lavender
ink.

༉

I swan.

A voice trails flickerings of tiny gold stars, yellow folds
of old thought, and cloth.

                                It comes through holes
an old veiled brilliance, toneless,

                        without acolyte
                        yet. This scuffle

    here for power that speaks.

                        ॐ

Daddy's out there praising the audacity of an earthly death.

She sings sometimes incoherently.

                        Blue Moon.
                Glimpsed in an orchard of pomegranates.

            He does not know of this, the king
            her father, too bad.

                The black pines
begin to silver at their tops and she walks around by herself,

                la, la, la, la.

PLACET FUTILE

I have zee heebie-jeebies.
Perhaps you shouldn't eat
that banana right now it's
gooing up your lipstick.

I was just thinking. Since
I am not him, where is that
little dog of yours, anyway?
You have very pretty hair.

No manure. It's like your laugh,
which is sacrilegious and
at the same time, innocent.

Here, let me tickle you
there. On the couch. Take
off your shoes, my darling.

AUTRES POEMES ET SONNETS

I.

I loved it
when the whole night
was found out
and was openly

on fire. He's
dear: torch songs and smoke
from immortal
cigarettes,

who lives
inside
an ancient bedroom
unwarmed,

even it he comes
in from the corridor
with another
fallen blonde.

II.

The line stops
without flowers.

I don't believe two mouths
ever knew the same kiss
they seemed to have in common.

The vase just sits there with
what it does not contain
in it.

PROSE

For Elaine

'High, purpley,' murmured Stephane. He was looking
up a word in the dictionary. Humming and Sighing.
This happened to him frequently. He couldn't spell.
Irretrievable time it seemed piled up like ironing.

Stephane was writing a story. Outside a breeze
rushed through the twilight and lilacs. It played
softly over his desk. He watched the sky fade
and first stars rise above the tops of palm trees.

'Oh, look!' Stephane's sister – a slim, utopian
girl – stood with her back to the landscape. (Wild
forsythia and the white surrounding oleanders.) He
thought of the world, and then the world of her.

'Uh oh,' Stephane remarked. It was a yellow
summery day in the life of the author. He went on,
'The mind writing about itself is the absence
of flowers – it notes – and presently troubled.'

Thus Stephane slept in a bed of a hundred irises.
It was funny. I don't know really if it ever
existed. It was somewhere down south. A little
place to remain nameless. Except for a hint:

it's on an island. 'The flowers are freer here,'
Stephane explained. 'You avoid the cost of making
them up when you can look right at them in person.'
Saying that, Stephane noticed how the flowers

all were commonly adorned with clear outlines.
He thought: the space between them is also
a space between them and the garden itself – the
distance of a space – which waves hi at us.

Stephane's children spent their summers on
the island. They were like clear ideas to him.
The faces of a disk, spinning in sunlight.
They went for walks, cooked, spoke English.

That is with the exception of his sensible sister.
Tenderly, she declined, and would go no further than
to spare a smile. She had always been the bright
one. Stephane made things up to understand her.

He made up a stalk of asphodels. That greeny flower.
It was too tall though, taller than reason grew, anyhow
Stephane's. Still he left it as it was. It was late,
and a spirit of contention shivered in the air.

Meanwhile, the shore wept. Waves in monotonous
succession wrote white lines of prose.
Stephane's childhood dog, Sandy, barks at them
harmlessly, and at Stephane. You can just hear him.

Beside a glittering sea, Stephane is caught
between the sky and the map. A wave ebbs
away. His footsteps in the sand attest to his
complexity. 'This island never existed,' he says.

Appozee, his sister, drove back to the mainland
over the boring bridge between it and the island.
'For garden seed,' she said, and thought: he was
born to be a goddamn book. That was Stephane.

Like their silly names, their love for each other.
It is an effort for Stephane to say this.
He stands watching the car as it retreats
across light green fields, somewhere in France.

IV.

BACKLIT

A species of
survival
assembles its
colored wings.

Something something
in the lanced air.

The unforeseen branch
syntax flutter
of what wasn't
and then is.

They use it
like a meaning:
it means
they are alive.

HOLDING GALATEA

He had to stop
making her up.

She was no longer
the outward form

of an ideal: she
was its portal into

the world. They were
a part of time. Her voice

echoed over a
transparent past.

She was more perfect
than anything he'd

intended. Life –
root and flower – was like

a thought she wore
in her hair.

ॐ

It swept him out into
depths beyond

desire itself. Nothing
had an adherence

to boundary – space,
gravity's semblance

of surrender, years
linked like intervals

of air.

༄

She awoke to his touch
again and again. Each was

the other's sun
and moon. But then

one day she wanted
to be on her own.

Light turned to stone
in her eyes.

He tried but couldn't
change her mind.

At the airport she waved
with one small hand

and disappeared past
the security gate. He

saw her again in
the crowd at the far

end of the hall, her face,
her bright winter coat.

NECESSARY SORROWS

Lorenzo died today. Or yesterday.
The obit was forwarded to me. Out
on the water small waves tent into
peaks of undulant light. All
you can see in Algeria is the green
immediacy, the mule and the wagon,
the war. Affection is a wandering
soul. A girl ends up being tall and
intelligent, with memories. If you
talk to yourself, don't forget her.

A PLACE

For Mary Farley

In prairie grass
the bleached flanks of

invisible muscle make
a prowling motion. Out

the windows of the bar
landscapes line up –

three of the same thing.
It seems you've won.

Now they're making
plans to go, old

lionesses of air, down
a dry dirt road.

THE LESSON

Proof against
a painted reprieve

lamentations
victims, ghosts

sullen color
ordained as virtue

flattens into
itself. Hallways

lead back to
the dead

half-comic order
of it's over

bound in listless
circles of

return. Sheets
slide along the

empty walls,
a white past.

THE IRINA POEMS

I. UNTIL

The watch is slipped off
with unceremonious candor.

This is going to get in the way.
What kind of wine is there?

The tearing and burrowing.
Flame-pointed stars circle

in opposite directions. Time
for the wallpaper report: roses,

yellow on blue, sir. I lean
against the brink of myself.

You breathe it in her hair.
You say it once too often.

2. A SHAME

'The sun at night is
a visible ball of

unraveling yarn.' She slips
on the frozen earth

beneath a soft layer
of still falling snow.

Atmosphere divides her.
A girl in green with

skates over her shoulder,
auburn-haired,

age eleven. The ice in
her mind shifts. Bears move

concealed behind
silver trees—

dark forms that follow
her everywhere.

3. STRABISMUS

Two days pass, the vessel
of belief is a pewter sieve.

Windows with gray May sky,
the park, the reservoir

dotted with white gulls,
everywhere I look

I see the same
willowy silhouette,

the cartoon pupils of
my eyes like Goofy.

4. MUSIC
After Blok

The alarm subsides.
At night the city starts to vanish.
God's music is: all the sounds
that earth can bear.

'I'll sweep shawl about my shoulders and face storm.'
You are, for me, the flame of roses,
the slanted sunlight at dusk
that fills the room.

Proprietor of the universe,
sing me the little tune
of pulse, of pain, of lovers
ending in oblivion.

5. THE MAD GIRL

She steps into the flame,
black eyes wide open.
Everything proceeds
from a single isthmus—

wave of momentary
error, secrets, witnesses,
Russia with its salt
butter of metaphors

spread over the cuts. Her
head hurts. The details
of despair, old as a beard,
ask beyond themselves

to be extended, impelled
to move again through
the indigo shadows of
snow, bells tinkling.

6. TONIGHT

Useless fustian voice

let her sleep.

7. UNKNOWN

Written on the tomb:
duration is irrelevant.

Welcome to the cremation.
We were an ideal,

ethereal, third and last.
The flames rose

like moans of
flamingoes.

8. REPLY TO RAIN

You're too willing to be
gravity's prize. Start from

the bottom, past moods like
misapplied colors, the names

of horrors – a riser's height–
up the stairscape of yourself.

Dust falls in the lamp's circle.
I don't want to solve or

change your life. If I did
I don't anymore.

9. A SMALL FIRE

A small fire remains
in the grate
wringing its hands.

ACKNOWLEDGMENTS

The New Yorker: 'Dinner,' 'Camera Obscura'

The Paris Review: 'The Rain Dragon,' 'Winter Nights,' 'Revenant'

Open City: 'Midnight,' 'Saltwater,' 'The Tin Room,' 'Science'

Backwoods Broadsides: 'The Climb'

Monkey Puzzle: 'Impasse'

Ekphrasis: 'The Drawing,' 'The Artist's Wife-to-Be'

Turtle Point Press Magazine: 'The Train'

Pyramid Editions: 'L'Après-midi d'un faune'

Marmalade (chapbook): 'Quelle Soie,' 'Hérodiade,' 'Placet Futile,' 'Autres Poems et Sonnets,' 'Prose'

Live Mag!: 'The Visible Leaf,' 'Music'

Forge: 'The Lawrence Snake,' 'Steps,' 'Sagaponack Notebook,' 'Until,' 'Away'

Local Knowledge: 'The Country Road.' 'Tree Trunks'

WILLIAM BENTON grew up in a small town on Galveston Bay. He received his early training in music and worked as a jazz musician before becoming a writer. His poetry has appeared in *The New Yorker*, *The Paris Review*, and other magazines. He is the author of a number of books, including *Exchanging Hats*, on the paintings of Elizabeth Bishop, and *Madly*, a novel. His most recent book is *The Mary Julia Paintings of Joan Brown* (Pressed Wafer). He lives in New York City.

This book has been set in Joanna Nova Book,
a type originally designed by Eric Gill.
Design & typesetting by Jonathan Greene.
Printing & binding by Thomson-Shore, Inc.